In the Mirror

Story by Joy Cowley
Illustrations by
Deirdre Gardiner

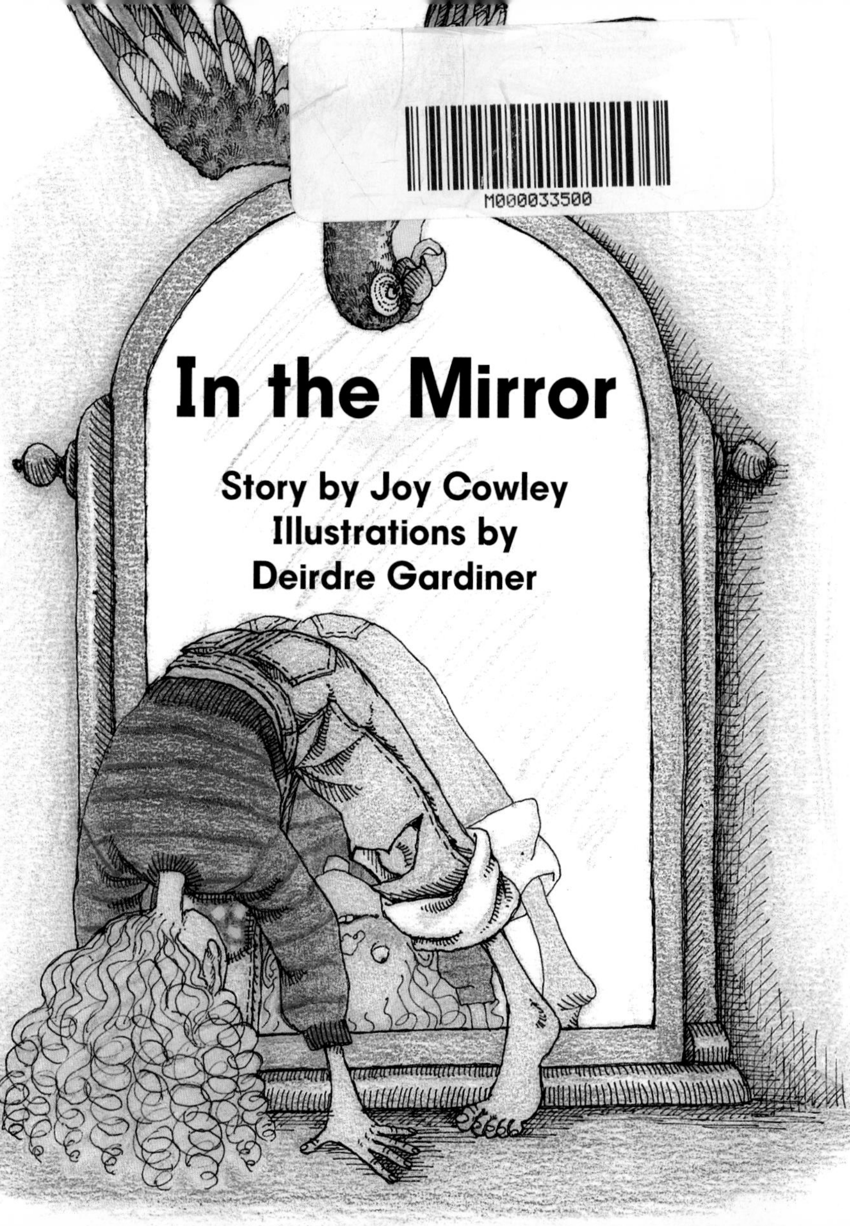

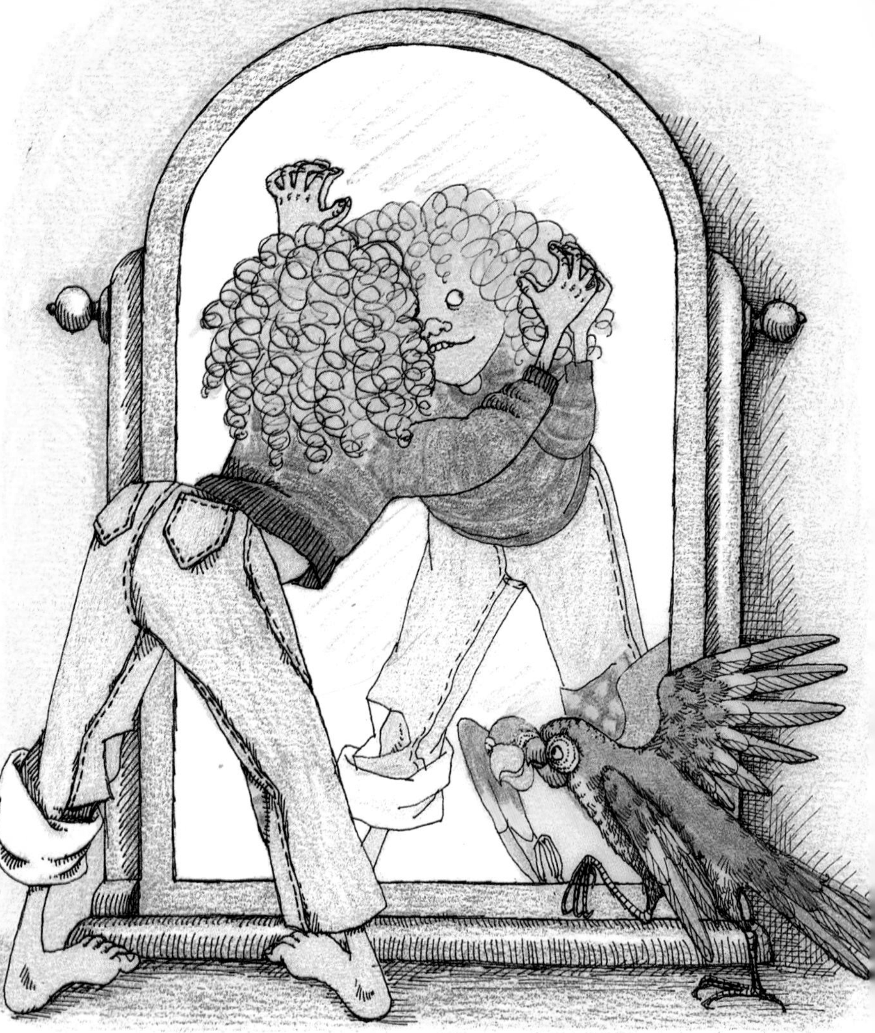

See my fingers.

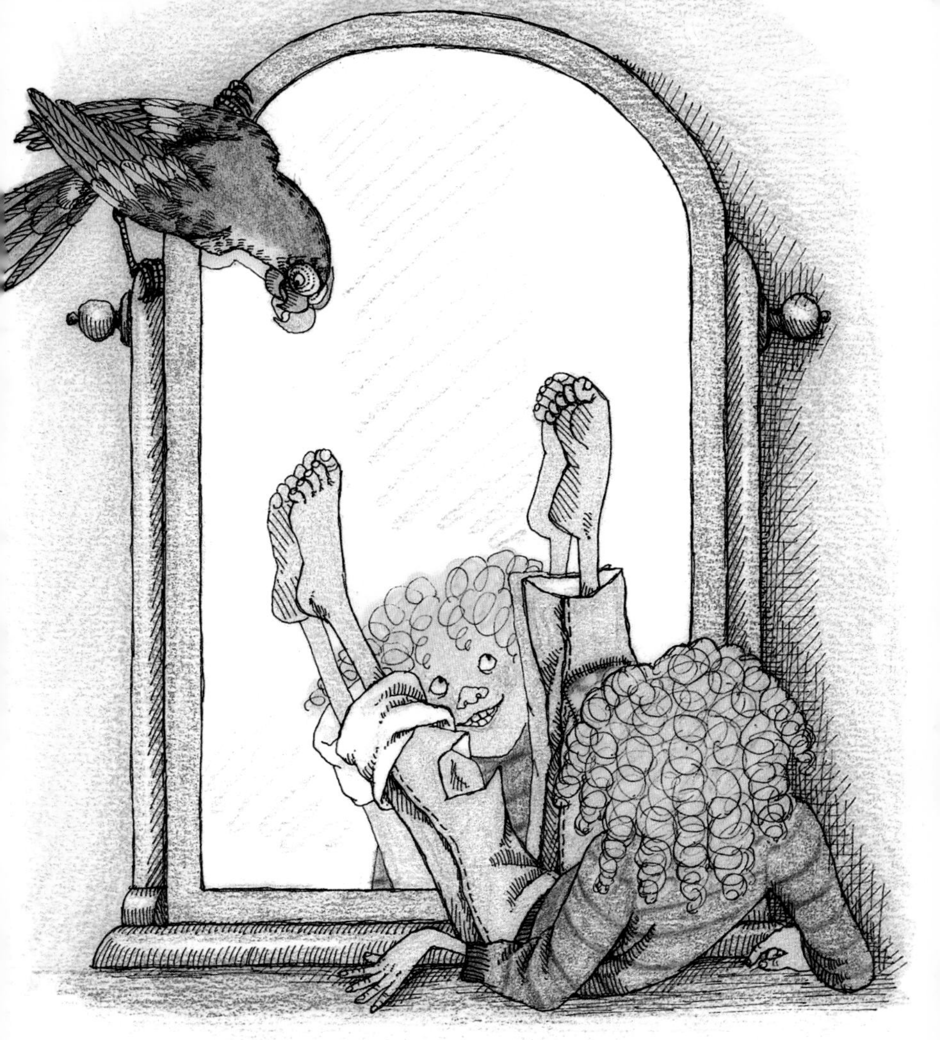

See my toes.

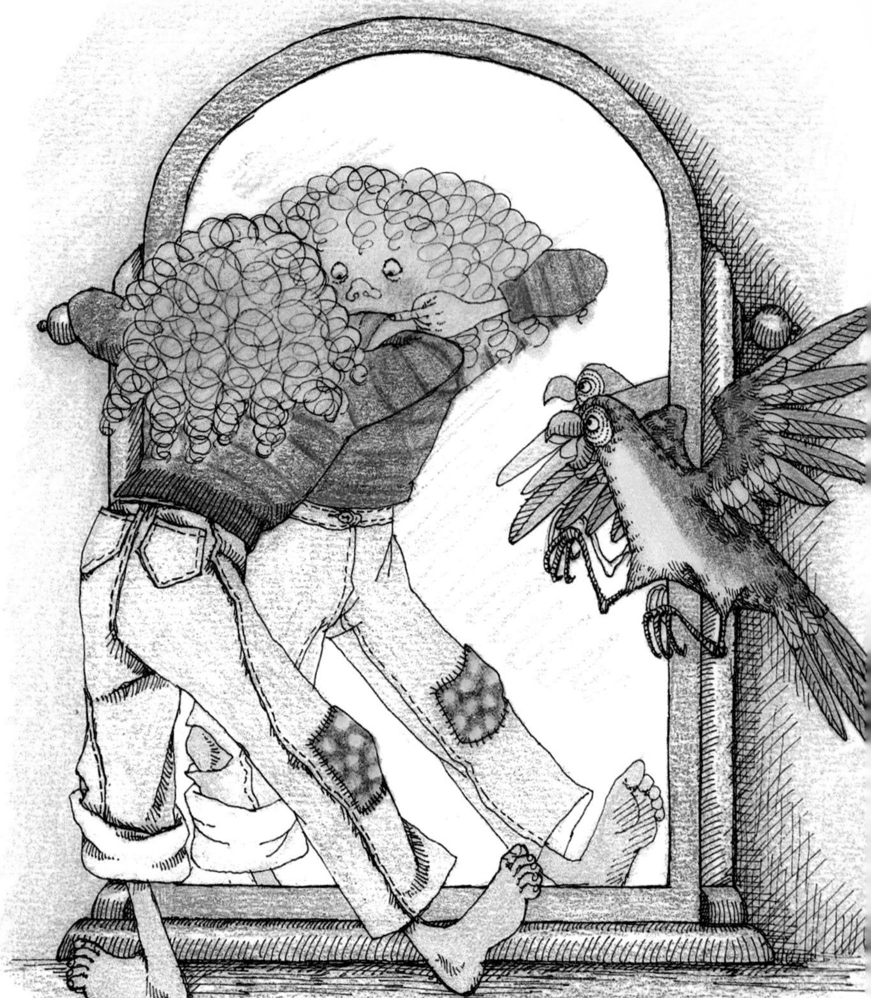

See my tongue.

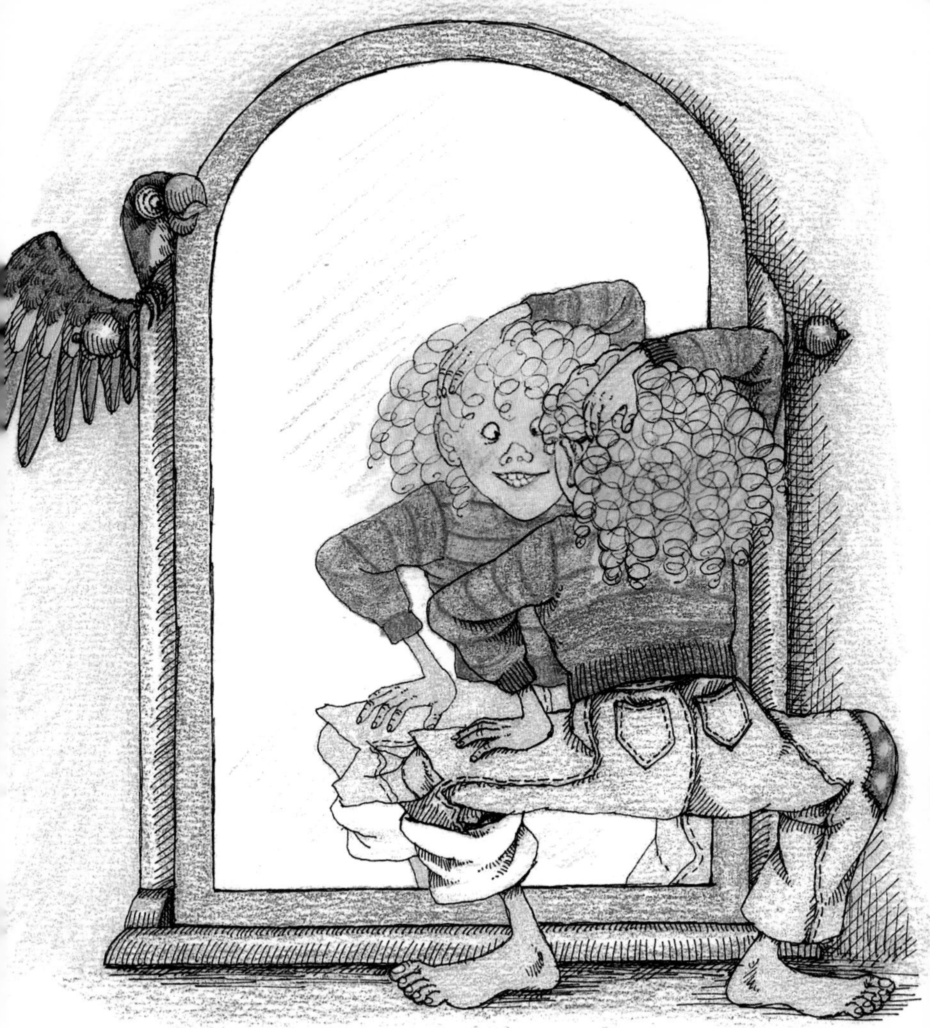

See my nose.

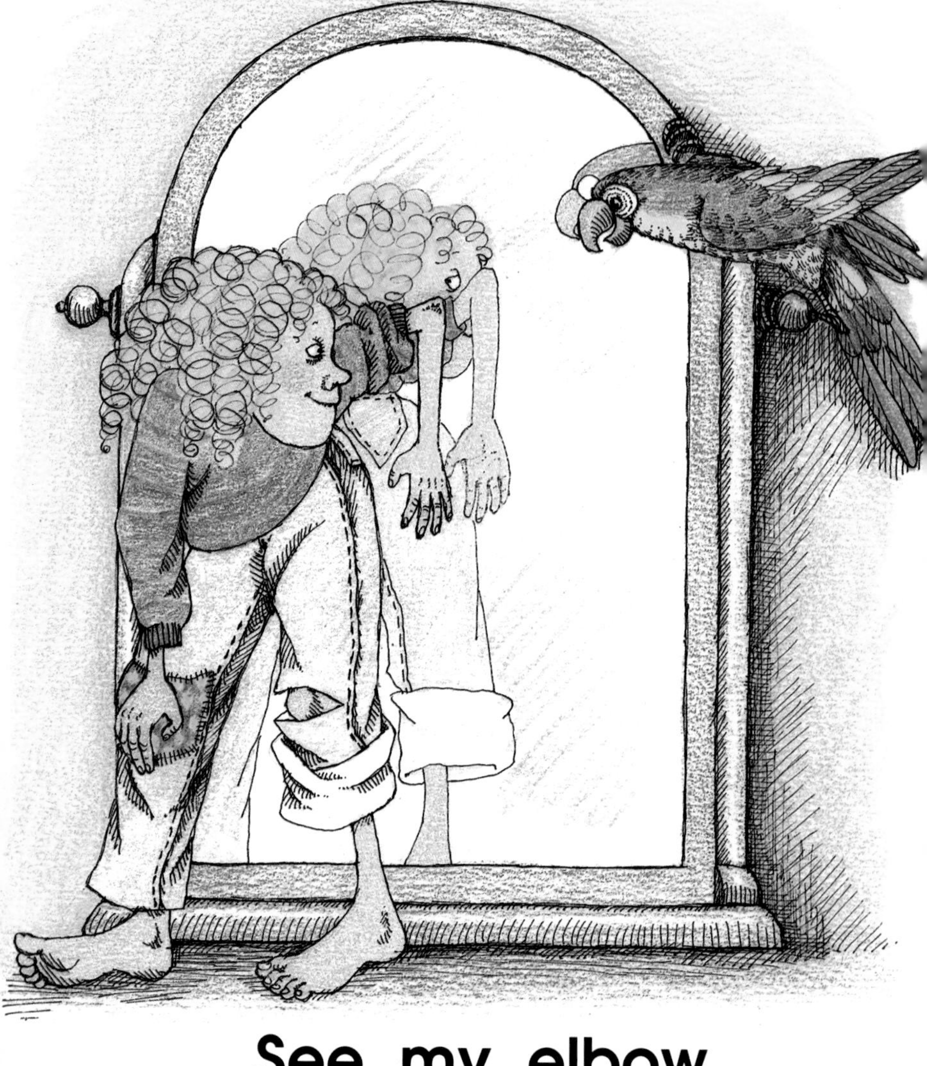

See my elbow.

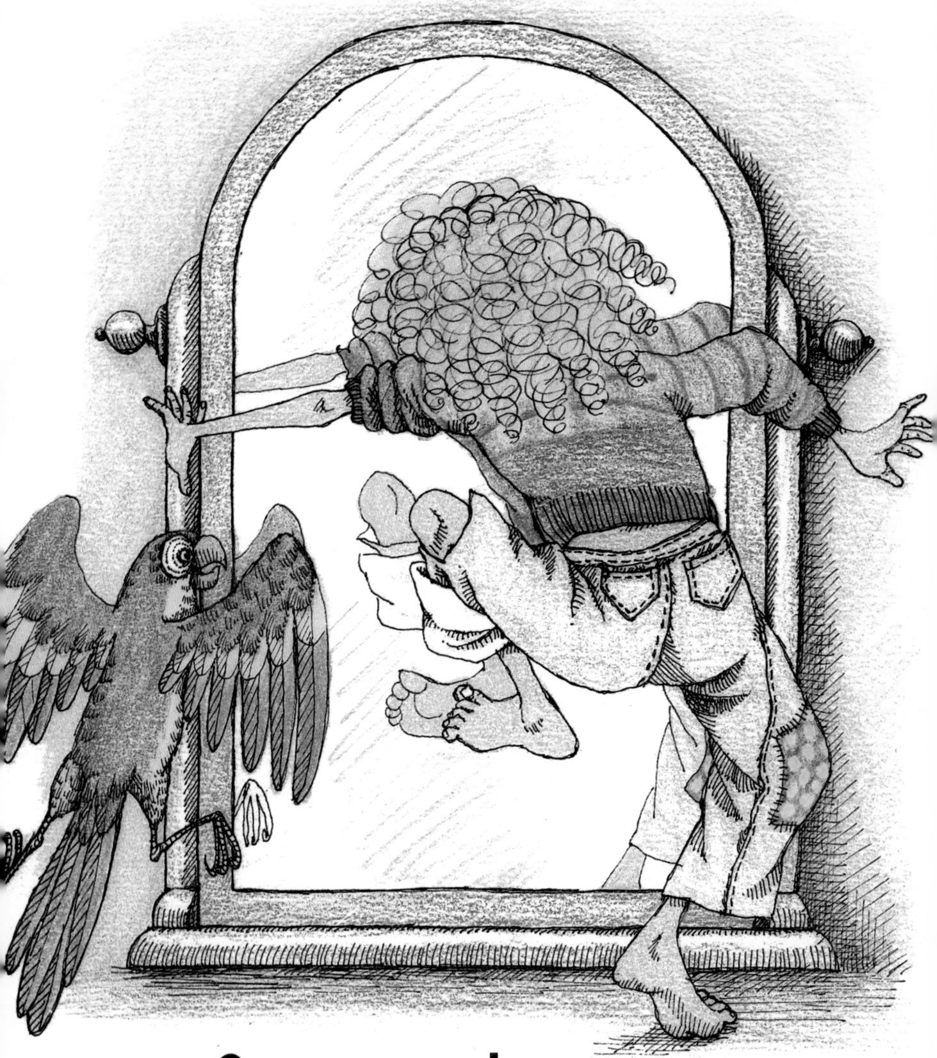

See my knee.

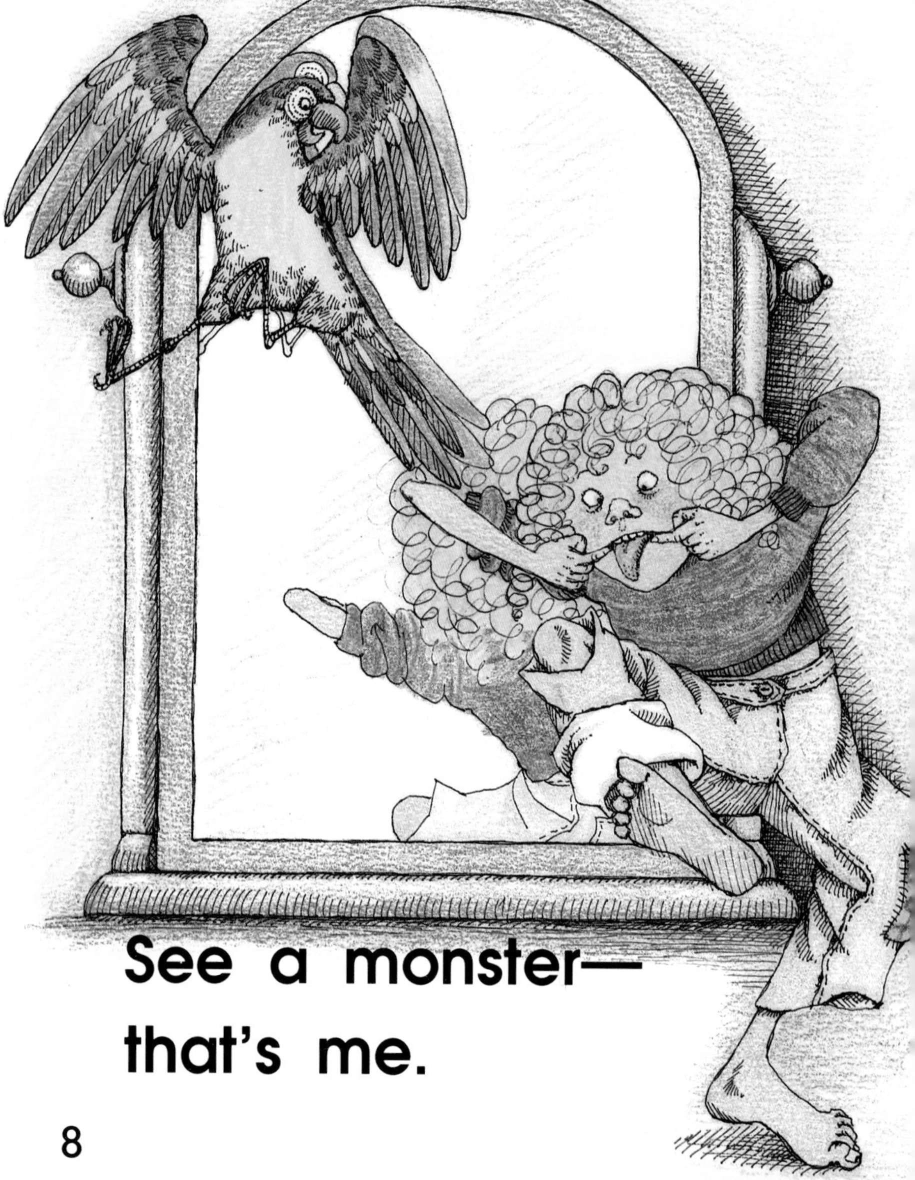

See a monster—
that's me.